The Positive Effects of utilizing

# Conflict Management
### In Life and Business Scenarios.

# JIMMY CHUNG

## Cover Illustration by Sarah Jeanne Chung

authorHOUSE®

*AuthorHouse*™
*1663 Liberty Drive, Suite 200*
*Bloomington, IN 47403*
*www.authorhouse.com*
*Phone: 1-800-839-8640*

*First published by AuthorHouse     7/16/2007*

*ISBN: 978-1-4343-1929-6 (sc)*
*ISBN: 978-1-4343-1930-2 (hc)*

*Printed in the United States of America*
*Bloomington, Indiana*

*This book is printed on acid-free paper.*

"Conflicts will continue to rise and fall, so the only solution is to keep producing solutions" – Jimmy Chung

# About the Author

Jimmy Chung was born into a low income family located in Queens County, New York. He was raised in an urban environment with limited opportunities. The parents of this individual realized that it would be difficult for him and his siblings to grow in such a restricted environment. They wanted to give him and his two sibling's space to grow and explore the world.

At the age of 12, Jimmy's parents decided to move the whole family out of their small apartment and into a house in the suburbs. He immediately took advantage of the various opportunities in his new surroundings. Jimmy for the first time had a backyard to play in. The backyard of his parent's home soon became his inspiration, which eventually turned him from an average boy to a man with big dreams. He had a main goal of using his backyard to either reduce or completely eliminate his asthma condition.

Jimmy did more than reduce his asthma condition to an extremely low level, but he started to have an interest in athletic activities. He knew weight lifting wasn't enough for him, so he decided to run and play baseball on a daily basis. Jimmy's hard work eventually paid off where he played two varsity sports, which included baseball and cross country long distance running. In the summer of 2003, Jimmy was scouted to an elite 16 and under baseball traveling team in New Jersey where he competed with his team in the U.S.A. Baseball Junior Olympic Championships tournament at a Major League Baseball Spring Training Complex. He was proud to turn a basic exercising routine into a chance to play under the watchful eyes of various Olympic and Major League Baseball scouts.

Jimmy had a personal goal of gaining academic success. He was able to develop from an average boy just sitting in the classroom into an active academic student. Jimmy graduated his high school with multiple honor cords, various medals/awards for his extracurricular activities, multiple community service awards, and a four year college scholarship.

Jimmy's academic success all started when he met his ninth grade global history teacher on the first day of high school. It was not a happy first meeting since Jimmy happened to arrive late in his teacher's class. He was scolded and warned by his teacher for showing up to class late, but little did Jimmy know that his teacher will eventually become one of his favorite mentors at Spring Valley High School. This global history teacher taught him how to achieve his academic and personal goals through various effective planning methods. Jimmy eventually was able to develop his own decision making skills from a novice level to tackling scenarios at the professional level. Chris Ferraro, a global history teacher and friend from Spring Valley High School, New York was the biggest influence on Jimmy's high school academic life.

Jimmy did not achieve his personal goals on just luck alone, but with various planning methods that he attained through experience. He depended on his ability to utilize critical thinking in almost any situation that he encountered. Most of his goals came with a blueprint, which allowed him to eliminate mistakes and improve his chances of turning dreams into reality.

In the present day, Jimmy Chung is a proud husband to Sarah Jeanne Chung (formerly McGrew) and father to Alana Amber Chung. He is an aspiring author and future entrepreneur. Jimmy wishes to develop future business opportunities and promote professional business ethic practices in the entrepreneur community. In his free time, Jimmy currently enjoys spending time with his family, exercising, playing baseball, writing, listening to music, and playing online video games.

This book was written based on Jimmy's personal experiences and knowledge to improve your decisions concerning life and business scenarios. You may seek additional information or contact Jimmy Chung by visiting his official web site at www.officialchung.com.

# Table Of Contents

# Preface

The author, Jimmy Chung takes readers to explore the mind of a critical alternative thinker in tackling the various conflicts established within our reality. The words "Life is unfair" has been repeatedly stated. There are many reasons why life is considered to be unfair. It is up to a person to establish a judgment, opinion, or ideas on a specific topic. Most people in society have the ability explore the uniqueness of their minds where fresh productive ideas can be extracted. This book is intended for individuals who wish to explore unique ideas, personal real life experiences, nonfiction scenarios, and advice on how to handle the various struggles in life.

Every person must realize that conflicts are all around us. We must face conflicts on a daily basis of 24 hours and 7 days a week. Some of us struggle in reality where some of us may also struggle in our sleep. You cannot avoid conflict as long as you are living in reality. It is possible to encounter situations when you set off to sleep. We cannot escape conflict and we never will. The world has established various conflicts where we must choose to produce solutions or run away from our problems.

The materials and content in this book will educate and enlighten you about the importance of making the most productive decisions. We must face various conflicts on a daily basis where it is possible to make mindless decisions. This book will allow you to make the most accurate and effective decisions. We are going to counter conflicts by taking critical thinking to the next level.

# Chapter One

## What is Critical Thinking?

- Defining the three main steps of critical thinking.

- Defining the three minor steps of critical thinking.

- Stating and applying the components of the critical thinking process.

# Chapter One

# What is Critical Thinking?

The power of critical thinking can take a problem solver to reach a variety of intelligence levels when solving conflicts. There are three main steps that form the structure and values of critical thinking. The first main structure requires a problem solver to identify the problem. The second main structure involves developing possible decisions and making a decision. The third main structure of critical thinking involves evaluating and placing the decision into effect. A person can increase their chances of gaining success by using all three structures.

## The Three Minor Steps and Components of the Critical Thinking Process

The concept of critical thinking can improve a person's decision making skills. Most businesses or organization use critical thinking in formulating marketing and advertisement plans. Some people may use critical thinking to analyze and acquire new knowledge. There are three minor steps as an addition to the three main structures of critical thinking. The three minor steps each plays an important role in the critical thinking process. The first minor step is to be aware that assumptions exist. The second minor step includes making assumptions accurate in order to produce positive effective results. The third minor step is to evaluate the assumptions. An assumption must make sense and provide some evidence for effectiveness. The assumptions should be evaluated for conditions that would determine the validity of ideas and resources. The critical thinking process is made of many various components. The major components of critical thinking include perception, assumptions, language, emotion, fallacy, argument, logic, and problem solving. These components each play a role in solving problems and providing solutions. There are many advantages of using the major components of critical thinking. The benefits of the critical thinking process can be applied in the personal, academic, and professional environment.

A person's perception can interfere with selecting plans or making decisions. The critical thinking process teaches people to be more open minded. It is important to look and evaluate more than one side of an argument. A person may learn new knowledge that can assist them in proving their points. Some people may discover the errors in their plans and goals by applying critical thinking into their problem solving procedures. The concept of critical thinking allows people to make assumptions. An assumption in critical thinking can outline and produce potential new ideas that may produce positive results. The language component involves persuading the audience through a detailed explanation with supporting evidence. A respected journalist for example must support their questions and ideas with facts or valid information.

The emotion component can be used to attract interest from an audience. Some journalists use their personal experiences and emotions to demonstrate how they can relate to a specific subject. The expression of emotion may provide enough supporting evidence to an audience.

The fallacy component is important in producing positive and effective results. It is important to evaluate multiple resources for the validity of information. Some resources may provide false information where the results would be inaccurate. The author and resource must be able to back up their information with supporting evidence. An accountant for example must depend on true numerical information when producing reports for a company. The numbers must be accurate to avoid producing false information that may cause a company to lose money.

The components of critical thinking are all important in assisting a person with the decision making process. A person can increase the possibility of producing effective results by evaluating resources and information for validity. It is important to use accurate material which may include facts from a creditable resource. The benefits of critical thinking include the ability to evaluate, develop, and effectively produce truthful information.

# Chapter Two

# What is the problem?

- Identifying a problem.

- Defining and outlining the current situation.

- Identifying an immediate threat.

- Identifying a potential threat.

- Create and state your objectives.

- Evaluate the effect produced from a problem.

# Chapter Two

# What is the problem?

We must deal with many conflicts on a daily basis where decisions must be made in order for any actions to occur. The only way to create an answer to a problem is to first identify the conflict. This is where the question "what is the problem?" comes into mind. A person cannot solve or provide an answer to a problem if they are not aware of the actual problem. It is possible to create an answer for a problem without actually acknowledging the contents of a situation. The negative down side of establishing a decision or answer without realizing the factors of a problem may lead to producing an inaccurate answer.

What is the point of producing an inaccurate answer? Do you want the best answer or one of the worst answers? I bet you want the answer that will produce the most accurate and effective results. We do not want the answer that fails to solve our problems. We only want the answer that has value and importance to be able to produce positive results. Most people believe that they fully understand the negative features of a situation. Some people believe they can fix a problem by establishing a quick decision. A quick decision can be used to solve a similar problem that was dealt in the past. The only negative downside of making a quick decision is that all problems may not be the same. A problem may appear to be similar, but it can be filled with various scenarios.

## What is the current situation?

Yes! We all know that a problem is causing a negative situation to occur. The problem may be bothering you all the day. You may be very eager to solve the problem right away. I want you to stop right there. You as the problem solver must be able to ask questions and answer your own questions before attempting to develop an answer. I will elaborate to avoid the confusion. An individual must ask themselves several questions that will contribute to the identification of a problem. A problem solver must outline the facts of the current situation. What is the current situation? The factual information of a situation should be collected and outlined before the thought of a potential answer.

## Is the problem an immediate threat?

It is understandable for a person to make a quick decision regarding a dangerous life or death situation. A life or death situation is a scenario where a person is faced to make a decision under limited conditions. An example of a limited condition would include a situation which requires a quick decision to be made under a short time period.

It is not understandable for a person to make a quick decision regarding a situation which may not be an immediate threat. A person who chooses to solve a question must first determine whether a situation is considered an immediate threat or potential threat. An immediate threat can cause harm or negative effects which may not be repairable. A problem with an immediate negative effects or threats may need quick decisions to be made in a small amount of time. Here are two examples of problems that pose as an immediate threat and require quick decision making:

## Situation One

Johnson decides to take a peaceful walk with his dog around the neighborhood. The neighborhood was nice and quiet until he heard a loud scream. The screaming contained the word help which was repeatedly being shouted throughout the neighborhood. Johnson decides to run toward the screaming sounds to figure out who was screaming and what was happening. In front of Johnson was an elderly woman trying to breath through the smoke that was coming out of her windows. The elderly woman's house was on fire where the front door was covered with debris. Johnson makes a quick decision to smash the windows and help the elderly woman out of the house.

## Situation One Analysis

Johnson had several options in this situation. He could have ignored the elderly woman completely by continuing with his walk. The second option would include calling the local fire department to save the woman and put out the torching house. The third option would include saving the woman himself. Johnson took the third option under the strict limited time conditions of the burning house. He took upon himself to make the best and effective decision in this scenario. The house in this case is obviously less important than the elderly woman. Johnson made a quick decision based on his personal observations of the situation. The elderly woman may have died if Johnson chose to ignore her. The second option of calling the fire department may have been too late to save the elderly woman.

## Situation Two

Amy is a hardworking high school student who balances academics, athletic activities, and academic clubs. She has a goal of building up her high school resume with multiple extracurricular activities to impress her desired colleges and universities. Most of the students in Amy's class admired her abilities to handle multiple school related activities. Amy was successful due to her ability to create and manage a well detailed daily schedule.

Amy always attended all her after school activities until she was eventually presented with a tough situation. Amy's debate team advisor decides to tell Amy that her team must entered into a last minute debate in order to qualify for the local championship. This event happens to be on the same day that Amy is scheduled to pitch for her softball team. The two events are scheduled at the same time where the locations are 40 miles apart. Amy is aware that the debate is a qualifying competition for the local championship where her softball game was just an exhibition game. She decides to make the ultimate decision of notifying and apologizing to her softball coach about the current situation. The softball coach understood the situation and decided to allow Amy to participate in the debate competition.

## **<u>Situation Two Analysis</u>**

Amy in this case chose the best decision based on her two options. The two options were to either play in the softball game or compete in the debate competition. She couldn't attend both events since they were both on the same day and time. The locations between the two events were too far apart for Amy. She made a personal decision of choosing to participate in the debate since it was considered more important. She had the chance to bring her debate team into the local debate championship. The softball game was just a normal exhibition game which was not as important in this case. The situation would of have been different if the softball game was a championship game and the debate event was only a normal debate.

The two situations reflect quick decision making. Johnson and Amy were placed in two different scenarios where the two individuals used their present knowledge to make the best decision possible. Johnson based his decision on observation and Amy based her decision on factual information. The two situations contained immediate threats where a time restriction played a role in forcing Johnson and Amy into making quick decisions.

# Is the problem a potential threat?

A problem that poses a potential threat should be carefully evaluated. It is important to identify whether a problem is an immediate threat or a potential threat. A potential threat does not carry a strict time restriction compared to an immediate threat. Most potential threats have an extended time period which may range from a few months to a couple of years. A potential threat requires time to build up. The event of a current immediate threat cannot be prevented since it has already occurred. A potential threat can be prevented or reduced by identifying the threat and developing procedures on how to handle the threat. Here is an example of a potential threat:

## Situation One

Sean lives in a beautiful Victorian house located in the countryside. The house is about twenty years old where it appeared to be in excellent condition. He was extremely proud of the low maintenance cost for maintaining the functions of his house. Sean never had to replace or fix anything in the house except for repainting his walls. He was shocked one day to find out that his outdoor deck appeared unstable. The wooden deck creaked and rumbled as he walked from one side to the other. Sean decides to make a decision of preventing the deck from collapsing by calling a general contractor for assistance. Sean and the general contractor discuss the best compatible deck to fit his house. The general contractor completely destroys the deck upon Sean's request and builds a new replacement deck.

## <u>Situation One Analysis</u>

Sean made the best decision according to his knowledge and personal preferences by replacing his old deck with a brand new one. The old deck presented a potential threat to Sean and anyone who decided to walk on it. Sean could have risked his own life as well as others if he decided to keep the deck. He had plenty of time to handle the situation where he consulted with a general contractor for advice and assistance. Sean even had the opportunity to choose the best deck to accommodate the size of his house. A potential threat situation allows an individual or group to handle a situation under an extended time period. The limitations on time are less restricted in a potential threat situation compared to an immediate threat scenario.

## Create and State your Objectives

The next step after identifying a problem is to create an outline of goals and objectives. You must figure out what you are trying to achieve. The goals and objectives would be related to your solution for solving a problem. You may risk the chance of creating an ineffective solution if you choose to make a decision without any real plans or goals.

A successful problem solver takes advantage of the brainstorming process to produce various objectives. There are many steps to take in figuring out the answer to a problem. A problem solver is recommended to create and place miniature goals into effect. The miniature goals are objectives that contribute to achieving a major goal. The accomplishment of a major goal usually in most cases requires an extended time period to achieve. Here is an example of creating miniature and major goals for a problem solving situation:

## <u>Situation One</u>

Sarah is a Human Resource manager for a local retail store. Some of her responsibilities include finding potential employees, hiring, provide employee training, enforcing company policies, regulating store activities, employee evaluations, and the termination of employees. She was always on task of recruiting employees to fill her store's employee quota. The store contained 10 different departments which required a maximum of 12 employees to be employed in each department. Sarah was always given plenty of time to fill and meet her company's employee quota until she received a message from her corporate office stating a new requirement. She was shocked to read the new company requirements. The company's corporate headquarters established a statement that required all Human Resource managers to recruit a minimum amount of 18 employees in total for each department by the end of two weeks. The new maximum total for hiring new employees into the company had increase from 12 to 25 employees for each department. The Human Resource managers of the company were now responsible for filling up each department with exactly a minimum of 18 employees. The company had also established a requirement which demanded that all Human Resources managers must complete their new employee quotas in the next two weeks.

This situation forces Sarah to take several steps in achieving her new goal of adding at least 6 new employees to each department. The addition of 6 new employees in each department would satisfy the new minimum requirement of 18 employees. The total number of new employees that Sarah must recruit into her store is 60 new employees.

She realizes that this task would require assistance from her store management team, so Sarah decides to establish a store meeting. The department management team is consisted of 10 department managers and 20 assistant department managers. Sarah takes advantage of her management team by asking all the department managers and their assistants to recruit 6 qualified individuals for an interview. The management team provides potential candidates for Sarah within a few days from her store meeting. The candidates all received interviews where all of them were qualified to be employed in Sarah's store. Every hired candidate received a new employee orientation and company training over the course of a few days. Sarah was able to complete her new employee quota by the company's deadline.

## Situation One Analysis

The company's corporate office in this situation forced a respected Human Resource manager to fulfill a difficult requirement. Sarah was placed to fill her employee quota in a time restricted environment. She was required to fulfill her employee quota of 18 employees for each department within a limited time period of two weeks. Sarah realized that the new company quota would be extremely difficult of fulfill by her deadline. She used her available resources which was the department management team. Sarah was able to established miniature goals for her department team. Every department manager and their assistants were encouraged to find at least 6 qualified candidates. The department managers were able to fulfill Sarah's miniature goals.

Sarah was able to fulfill her major goal of completing the company's deadline of two weeks by acting in her own procedures. The next steps involved interviewing and taking the necessary steps as a Human Resource manager to employ the new candidates. The new candidates were systemically trained and prepared to work by the company's deadline.

Sarah results were successful due to her ability organize and establish detailed goals. She was able to apply her knowledge of the company's deadline by formulating a step by step plan. A well skilled problem solver usually has the ability and work ethic to create a plan. It may be annoying to spend time brainstorming and developing a blueprint, but it is worth the time to produce positive and effective results.

The creation of objectives is an excellent source of guidance for various situations. It is always possible to lose focus on creating a solution. Sarah was able to stay on task and meet her deadline by focusing on the main objective. The establishment of goals provides the necessary steps for a problem solver to use in combating a conflict.

## Evaluate the Effects of a Problem

You have identified your problem and established the various objectives for developing a solution. The next step is to effectively evaluate the effects of a problem. You must create an outline with specific details concerning the effects of a problem. The results from a conflict can provide a problem solver with facts and information on how to approach a specific issue. A great problem solver must be able to observe, analyze, and record the effects from a problem in order to develop a solution for fixing a conflict.

# Chapter Three

## Framing Causes and Solutions

- Identifying the origination point of a conflict.

- Evaluating the possibility of multiple causes.

- Defining solution oriented goals.

# Chapter Three

# Framing Causes and Solutions

Every conflict that occurs has an origination point where a problem started. The origination point of a conflict can also be reference as the root cause of a problem. A problem solver that wishes to produce or find a solution to solve a conflict must be able to analyze and frame the conflict. You cannot solve a problem if you do not tackle or focus on producing solutions that will directly affect the root cause of a conflict. The framing concept of critical thinking is one of the most important tools to use in the planning process. The goal of critical thinking is to allow an individual to explore the fine details of a situation. You must use all your senses and abilities to locate and evaluate a situation in a step by step process. An individual that chooses to skip a step during the problem solving processes may increase the risk of producing inaccurate results.

## Identifying the Origination Point

The identification of a problem's origination point requires intensive studying and evaluation. A problem or conflict requires a catalyst to create the spark which produces the negative results. You can have a great chance of solving problem if you can figure out the root cause of a dilemma. There are two advantages of finding the source of a current or potential problem.     The first advantage of finding the origination point for a current conflict would include the opportunity to develop a better understanding of the issues involved. The second advantage of finding the origination point for a potential problem would include the ability to prevent an issue from occurring.

A person would have a slim chance of solving a conflict if they did not understand the problem. The origination point can offer and open many opportunities such as fresh ideas and potential solutions. A problem solver can base their plans and objectives on the root cause of an issue. It is important to evaluate and make sure that the origination point is valid and supported with factual evidence. You can make an assumption concerning the cause of an issue, but you have to be able to support your claims. An individual who chooses to base their entire plans, goals, solutions, and final decisions on an origination point without valid confirmation may risk producing inaccurate results. The most important component of critical thinking involves the ability to support your own claims without using fallacy information.

A great way to find the origination point of a conflict is to create an outline. This outline should state the negative results that formed the problem. A back track method would be useful in completing an origination point outline. The back track method involves a brainstorm session, which focuses on developing possible root cause ideas. This method requires an extensive amount of time in order to receive the most accurate results. You will be able to list and evaluate your possible origination point ideas before any actions or decisions are established. Here is a scenario that displays the identification process of finding the origination point of a problem.

## **Situation One**

Steven is a cashier who works for a local home improvement store. Some of his responsibilities include greeting the customer, providing customers with product knowledge, completing transactions, and assisting customers with bringing products into their cars. The company that he works for has provided him with basic company training. Every employee in his company must constantly attend training classes on a daily basis. The home improvement store has even established a monthly routine of holding store meetings. The store meetings provide the employees with information on how to improve their services and abilities. The home improvement company provides Steven and fellow coworkers with various resources on how to provide the best service possible. The resources and training however may not be enough to prepare Steven for every situation that he encounters.

Steven was working the cash register one day where he met a customer named Kathleen. He greeted Kathleen and completed her transaction. Steven decides to prepare himself to go on his lunch break until Kathleen comes charging back into the store to talk to him. She yelled with an enraged tone stating that she was overcharged for a set of 20 flooring tiles. Kathleen demanded Steven to provide her with a refund, so that she can be charged for the correct price.

The computer system in the home improvement store was frequently updated by the department managers, so the chances of the product pricing being wrong were slim. Steven has limited knowledge on flooring tiles since he does not work in the flooring department. He explains to Kathleen that he will do his best to assist her with correcting the price.

Steven decides to listen to Kathleen explanation of the price difference. Kathleen explains that she saw the set of 20 flooring tiles for a total of three dollars. She was charged 60 dollars for the set of 20 flooring tiles. Steven decides to take the next step by allowing Kathleen to take him to the flooring tile department. She shows Steven the sign which represented the price of the flooring tiles. The pricing sign and the flooring tiles were all placed in the proper locations. The prices of the tiles were corrected. The sign stated that each tile had a flat cost of three dollars. Steven had to notify Kathleen that the flooring tiles were 3 dollars each instead of the whole set.

## <u>Situation One Analysis</u>

A retail environment is filled with many surprises which may range from random customer questions to various transactions. Steven encountered a difficult situation where he used several steps to come with a solution. Kathleen assisted Steven with the first step of problem identification where she told him about the problem. Steven took the second step of establishing an objective, which involved finding the correct price for the flooring tiles. The third step was to conduct research where he asked Kathleen to take him directly to the flooring department. The fourth step was validation where he confirmed the correct price for the flooring tiles. Steven was able to prove to Kathleen that she misread the price sign. It is always important to confirm information for validity to avoid creating inaccurate results. Steven could have lost the company money if he chose to charge the set of flooring tiles as a total of three dollars instead of three dollars each.

## Evaluating the possibility of multiple causes

Some situations may contain more than one possible cause. There are situations where one single problem may have been caused by a series of contributing factors. The assumption that a problem has more than one cause can open new ideas. A problem solver who chooses to list multiple causes can increase their ability to come up with multiple solutions.

There are conflicts where the result of a problem can be caused by another factor. It is important identify multiple causes through a step by step process. The back track method in a multiple contributing factors case involves linking one factor to another factor in order to come up with possible solutions.

## Defining solution oriented goals

The most important step to figuring out an answer for a problem involves focusing and concentration. A problem solver must create an outline of their objectives and what they want to achieve. A conflict situation is considered incomplete since it requires attention and a solution. The identification and establishment of goals that focus on developing an answer for a problem would keep a problem solver on track. It is always possible to lose focus on a certain subject. The outline of objectives would be presented and used as a main reference resource. You can think of an objective outline as a step by step instructional map. A solution goal only focuses on developing possible solutions for a problem. An objective only focuses on creating miniature goals, which are used to develop possible solutions as mentioned in Chapter 2.

# Chapter Four

# Analyze and apply your decisions

- Create and analyze the impact of multiple potential solutions

- Choose your solution and make a decision.

# Chapter Four

# Analyze and apply your decisions

The final step of the critical thinking process involves producing results that will hopefully solve the problem. The process of developing multiple solutions is completed. The next step is to measure the impact of multiple solutions. A good problem solver would create an estimate or prediction of results may occur from their solutions. You do not know what results will the solutions produce, but you can make a prediction. A prediction of a solution's results can give a person a better idea of what events may occur.

## Create and analyze the impact of multiple potential solutions

The brainstorm process is a great concept to use in producing possible ideas. This process may be applied into developing ideas that may influence the creation of possible solutions. A problem solver can take advantage of the brainstorm process by developing more than one possible solution. It is always important to give yourself more than one choice. A single solution to a problem can only produce one result. The establishment and application of multiple solutions to a single problem can produce a number of various results. There will be situations where one solution may present more positive results than another solution. There will be situations where one solution may produce more negative results than another solution. Some situations may not allow you to witness all the potential results. An excellent solution evaluate whether one solution is better than another would involve making predictions. A prediction would give a problem solver an idea of what may happen if they chose to apply a specific solution. It is obvious to choose the solution that will produce a positive effect with the least amount of negative results. A prediction can assist a person in making the best choice out of a situation. It is all about comparing and contrasting between multiple solutions in a search to produce the best most productive results.

## Choose your solutions and make your decision

The next step after the solution evaluation process is to pick the best solution. The selected solution would be used as an answer for a problem. The solution should be placed into the most appropriate situation to receive accurate results. The last step of the critical thinking process is to apply your decision.

The results that may occur from your decision should be recorded in a final outline. The final outline can used to keep track of results for future references. You may encounter the same or similar situation in the future. The final outline would remind you of how you handled a specific situation. Here is an example of a situation involving a final outline:

## <u>Situation One</u>

Gary is a member of his elementary school's science club. This science club provides students the opportunity to receive hands on experience in the world of science. Some of the activities involve science lectures, indoor science experiments, and outdoor scavenger hunts. This club allows students to apply what they learned in the classroom into producing real life experiences. The elementary science club is not only fun and games. There are required assignments which must be completed on a weekly basis. The students are given a final science club exam by the end of the year. Most of the questions from the science club exam are based on the experiments completed throughout the entire year.

There was an event that required every student to build a model of a volcano. The main goal of the event was to produce a simulation of fake flowing lava. Every science club member was required to make fake lava flow out of their model volcanoes. Gary made several attempts to create a simulated erupting volcano. He created a realistic looking volcano, but he didn't know how to make fake lava. The first attempt of creating fake lava involved placing a plastic tube into the crater of the volcano with a manual pump filled with red dyed water. He was unfortunately unsuccessful since the pump shot the red water up into the air as a stream. The assignment required him to make the fake lava flow as realistic as possible.

Gary realized that he had to conduct some research on producing a simulation of fake lava. He decided to borrow a science experiment book from his school's library. The science experiment book described an experiment which involved exploding liquid into the air. The ingredients of the experiment included baking soda, vinegar, and a plastic bottle. The first step of the experiment was to pour the vinegar into the plastic bottle. The second step was to pour baking soda into the bottle. The final result of the experiment ended in an explosion of foam and liquid shooting out of the plastic bottle.

Gary knew that a volcano produces a similar effect where lava erupts out of the volcano. He decided to combine this experiment with his volcano. The only problem with the baking soda and vinegar was the color. The color of lava is usually red or orange. Gary realizes the problem and decided to combine the vinegar and red dye together. The next step was to place the baking soda where he was pleased to witness the fake lava flowing out of his simulating volcano. Gary realized that this experiment would be on the final exam so he decided to produce a step by step outline as a reference. He also created a solutions outline which represented all the possible solutions and results that he encountered.

## **<u>Situation One Analysis</u>**

Gary did not have enough knowledge to achieve his goal in the initial experimenting process. The only way to figure out a way for accomplishing his goals was to go through a series of trial and error. The experiments that did not produce positive results were eliminated from being used to present his experiment. The next step after eliminating his faulty ideas involved conducting research. He was able to take some time to conducted research on finding the best solution. The best solution in this case was the baking soda and vinegar combination, which he had found while researching. The success in this scenario was due to Gary's personal abilities to effectively search and find a compatible solution for his problem. He realized that the volcano experiment will be on the final exam so he took the final step of recording his findings in a final outline for future references.

# Chapter Five

# Friendship Conflicts

- How do I make friends?

- How to build trust.

- Participate in an internet community forum and make new friends.

- Join a club.

# Chapter Five

# Friendship Conflicts

The value of friendship can either be taken seriously or thrown into the garbage pile. It feels good to spend time with another person. You may have the same interests as the next person and sometimes you may be a complete opposite. Most people enjoy the company of others. A friend can provide emotional support when you are feeling low for the day. A friend can provide a reasonable amount of financial support if you cannot afford to pay for a slice of pizza. It is nice to have a friend, but some people are misfortunate. Some individuals in our society have a tough time making friends for various reasons. Some people just prefer to be alone for personal reasons. This chapter is designed to help any individual who wishes to find a friend.

### How do I make friends?

There are many different ways to make new friends. The achievement of making a new friend starts with the individual. You must be willing to go out and explore the world. The first step in making a friend is to identify your problem. The current problem is that you want a friend, but you do not currently have a friend. The second step involves defining your main objective which is to find a new friend. The third step is to evaluate and outline reasons why you do not currently have a friend. The next step of making a new friend involves identifying the cause of your problem. You must create an outline of why you do not currently have a friend. Here are some questions that you can ask yourself:

## Why do I want a friend?

There may be several reasons why an individual would want a friend. Some people do not like to be lonely, so instead they prefer to interact with other people. Some individuals enjoy the attention that they receive from other individuals. There are people in our society that depend on the company of others to enjoy their lives. Some people just want a friend to share their interest and hobbies with. You can go on to the next question once you can figure an answer for this question.

## Am I confident with my personal abilities?

This is an important question because it can determine whether you will make a new friend or not. You must be able to build your own confidence before approaching another person. There are several ways of building your confidence in your personal abilities. The first technique to building personal confidence would involve choosing an activity. This activity must be something that you are willing to do. You must either carry some interest or be willing to learn and develop an interest. Some examples of activities may include exercising, video games, hobbies, and other popular activities. It is important to build an interest in a popular activity since there are more opportunities to make friends with similar interest. You would decrease the chances of meeting a friend with compatible interest if you chose to participate in an unpopular activity. The obvious effect from an unpopular activity would include a small population that participates in the specific activity. You would be able to open many opportunities once you are able to define your own interest and build confidence.

## Am I assertive enough to approach another individual?

You cannot meet or make a friend if you are afraid to approach another individual. Some people are able to communicate with other people without any fear. Unfortunately, there are some people in our society that do have a fear when it comes to communicating with others. It is completely normal to be afraid to start off a conversation. Here are some of the most common fears when it comes to approaching another individual:

1) Are they going to tell me to go away?

2) Will they insult me?

3) We might not share the same interest.

4) I don't know what to talk about.

5) How do I start the conversation?

6) How do I get their initial attention?

7) I might scare them off.

8) Are they dangerous?

9) I don't think I can keep them interested in a conversation.

It's completely normal to think and worry about these fears before approaching another individual. The most important concept is to conquer and make attempts to ignore these fears. You have to live your life by exploring nature and your surrounding environment. You should not keep yourself isolated from the wonders of the world just because of your personal fears. It is important to remember that conquering your fears may take some time. Some people are able to conquer their fears in a small amount of time. Some people may require an extensive amount of time to eliminate their personal fears. It is possible for a person to take hours, days, weeks, months, or even years to eliminate their fears.

The only ways of conquering your fear is to conduct research and facing your fears. Here are some tips and advice on how to handle the most common fears when it comes to approaching another individual:

## Are they going to tell me to go away?

There may be a possibility that a person might tell you to go away. It is always important to remember that every person that you approach will carry unique personalities. Everyone is influenced by a variety of factors that may include family members, friends, the media, and other informative or influential resources. Some people might tell you to go away for a variety of reasons. Here are some of the reasons why a person might tell you to go away:

- An individual may have been taught as a child to avoid talking to strangers.

- An individual may have their own personal problems with socializing with other people.

- An individual may carry their own confidence issues.

- An individual may have faced a recent family or friend related crisis.

- An individual may have experienced a tough day at work.

You must remind yourself that another person may tell you to go away for various reasons. The fear of being insulted or rejected should not stop you from being sociable. You should take advantage of life's many opportunities. There is no reason for restricting yourself. It is recommended that you should approach a conversation with another individual in an appropriate environment. Some safe and neutral environments may include a restaurant, Neighborhood Park, education institution, or any other wide open public environment. You should always use your personal safety knowledge and abilities to avoid encountering a dangerous environment.

## Will they insult me?

The chances of somebody insulting you for no apparent reason in a public place are usually slim. It is your own personal responsibility to develop and make a clear judgment of others. There are situations when you can tell that someone prefers to be left alone. Some people may just have a terrible personality where they enjoy insulting others around them. You can make attempt to avoid being insulted by another person by evaluating their behavior. A person's facial expression and tone of voice can reflect an individual's personality. There are many people in this world to meet, so you do not have to restrict yourself to meeting only one person. It is recommended to avoid individuals that you believe to be potentially hostile.

## We might not share the same interest

You will never know whether someone shares the same interest as you if you do not approach a conversation with another person. Our world and society provides many opportunities.

There are only two results that exist in our reality. You can either produce positive results or fail and produce negative results.

It is important to remember that everyone in the general public is unique by personality. You do not need to have the same interest in order to be friends with another person. There are plenty of friends and couples who may carry the complete opposite list of interest. Some people may listen to a specific genre of music, but may not listen to the same bands. There are many reasons why people become friends so you do not have to worry sharing the same interest with another person.

## How do I start a conversation if I don't know what to talk about?

A situation can be difficult if you do not know what to talk about. There are several ways of tackling this situation. The first step involves evaluating the person that you wish to speak with. An observation of a person's clothing and actions may provide you with ideas on what to talk about. The second step will require you to greet the person by either saying hello or excuse me. These greetings act as an ice breaker between you and the person that you are interested in talking with. The third step will require you to pick a result from your observation and talk about it. Here are some small examples of using your observations skills to create a conversation:

*Example One*

Ryan walks into a college library and notices one of his classmates. The classmate happens to be a girl that he has an interest in talking with. Ryan has not had the chance to formally introduce himself, so the classmate has no idea who he is. He decided to walk toward her and introduce himself. Ryan even took the opportunity to tell his classmate that he was in her class.

The fact that they shared the same class allowed Ryan to start a conversation about lectures relating to their class.

The next step involved Ryan's ability to observe the appearance of his classmate. She was wearing a shirt with a picture of a well known popular music artist. He took the opportunity and asked her questions about the music artist on her shirt. The classmate carried the conversation by describing her music interest which led him to describe his own interest.

*Example Two*

Mary Ann is physically active college student who enjoys working out at the college gymnasium. She was walking to the treadmill room one day where she noticed a man wearing a martial arts uniform. Mary Ann was always interested in learning martial arts, so she decided to approach the individual.

She introduced herself by stating her name and that she was interested in learning martial arts. Mary Ann continued the conversation by asking questions concerning the man's martial arts practice. The individual was happy enough to explain to Mary Ann of the philosophies concerning his martial arts practice. The two carried a conversation which led Mary Ann to meet her future personal martial arts trainer and friend. Mary Ann had no previous experience or knowledge concerning martial arts where the man was an experience martial artist. The two individuals in this case were able to start and carry a conversation even though their knowledge on a particular topic was different from each other.

## Are they dangerous?

It is always important to meet someone in a general public place to decrease the chances of physical violence from occurring. You may be able to sense or tell whether someone is potential dangerous. An observation of a person should automatically tell you whether you should approach a certain individual or not.

## I don't think I can keep them interested in a conversation

The most important thing in trying to make a new friend involves starting a conversation. You should start a conversation and see how things will go from there. You will never know the results if you do not engage in any actions. It is up to you to decide whether to carry the conversation further or stop.

## How to build trust

The developing process of building and establishing the subject of trust in a friendship may be one of the most difficult steps to accomplish. Everyone has their own abilities and qualifications for determining whether a specific individual is trustworthy or not. There are certain individuals or groups that are usually considered trustworthy in our modern day society. Some of the most common trusthworty individuals or groups may include parents, grandparents, siblings, best friends, teachers, coaches, and personal professional advisors. There are many reasons why these individuals are more likely to be trustworthy compared to a stranger. The main reason would be the fact that most family members, teachers, coaches, and professional advisors have a personal interest in our abilities. These individuals may play a huge role in your development into a respected person in modern society.

It may be difficult to trust a new friend for several reasons. A new friend may not have the chance to prove to you that he or she is trustworthy. The relationship between you and the person that you just met is considered a novice relationship. A novice relationship is an inexperienced connection between two individuals. You may not contain the knowledge of a person's history. A person's history or past activities may play a role in determining whether someone can be considered trustworthy or not. Here are some steps on how to develop a trusting relationship with a friend:

*Step 1*

### Identify the problem

I want to be able to trust my friend. How can I build a trusting relationship with my friend?

*Step 2*

### Define main objective

The main objective is to build a trusting relationship between me and my friend.

*Step 3*

### Define mini objective(s)

- Learn more about your friend's history.
- Learn more about your friend's family.
- Learn more about your friend's other influences besides you.

*Step 4*

### Evaluate the effects of the problem

- You do not currently trust your friend.
- You cannot develop a strong friendship.
- You may find it difficult to talk about your personal life with your friend.

*Step 5*

## Identify the causes of the problem

- The time period of your relationship between you and your friend is relativity new.
- You or your friend hasn't had the opportunity to prove his or her loyalty to each other.

*Step 6*

## Create possible solutions

- You and your friend may require an extended time period to develop a trusting relationship.
- You and your friend may want to participate in activities which require actions involving teamwork.
- You and your friend should spend more time doing various activities such as your favorite hobbies.
- Learn about you friend's history, family structure, and influences.

*Step 7*

## Evaluate impact of solutions

- The selection of an extended time period may decrease the ability to form a trusting relationship.
- The participation of activities that involve teamwork would present the opportunity to create and form a strong bond.
- A favorite hobby or activity can play a major role in the development of a trustworthy relationship.
- A friend may be able to build trust in another friend by researching and learning about their history. You may gain

a better understanding of your friend by evaluating their personal influences.

## *Step 8*

### Select a solution and made a decision

- The solution that may potentially create positive results in this case is the extended time period solution.
- A friendship may require a long period of time to develop trust between two individuals.
- An extended time will allow a friendship between two individuals to learn and eventually trust each other.

## *Step 9*

### Evaluate the impact of your decision

- An extended time period can allow a friendship to grow where each friend will have the opportunity to learn more about the other person.
- The impact of this decision would give two individuals the opportunity to encounter similar experiences.
- An extended time period provides individuals the opportunity to gain truthful knowledge about their friends.

## *Step 10*

### Place your decision into effect

- The final step involves building a friendship over a course of an extended time period.
- An extended time period for a friendship to grow and develop trust may range from weeks to many years.

- A decision should always be placed into the most appropriate situation.
- You have a responsibility as a friend to notify your friend of concerns involving trust issues.
- The discussion of recognition involving trust issues

## Participate in an internet community forum

We currently live in a technology dominated environment. Our society has become more dependent on advanced modern day technology. The advancement of technology has opened new doors which are filled with many opportunities. The internet is an excellent resource for learning new information, developing social skills, and making new friends. There are so many advantages of using the internet as a source for building confidence. You can talk to almost anyone in the world just by sitting in front of the computer. There are many advantages of talking online. The internet provides many communication opportunities, which may be used for personal or professional reasons. You can speak or communicate with another individual without seeing their face. The availability and opportunity of chatting online with people around the world can boost your personal confidence. You may be able to learn something new from the internet. There are many various information oriented websites that provide individuals the opportunity to learn and discuss their opinions. Most information websites provide their viewers with a community forum or blog.

The creation of the community forum has allowed internet users to learn new information, express their personal opinions, and socialize with other individuals. A community forum is usually filled with individuals that may share the same interest. A group of individuals that may share the same interest would create an opportunity to make new friends.

There are many advantages of researching, selecting, joining, and becoming an active member of a community forum. Here are ten advantages of joining a community forum:

## Ten advantages of joining a community forum

1) A community forum is usually created for individuals that may share similar views, interests, and opinions on a particular subject.

2) You do not have to meet anyone physically in a community forum.

3) You can express your opinions in a controlled and stabled environment.

4) There may be others that are willing to support your ideas and beliefs.

5) You can collect personal opinions from being people around the world by establishing internet surveys or polls.

6) You can build your social abilities by constantly interacting with other individuals through debates and normal discussions.

7) Read and learn from various experiences expressed by other individuals.

8) Some community forums may create physical events where you can actually attend social events.

9) A community forum would allow you to see more than one perspective concerning any specified topic.

10) You can post questions and receive advice from a variety of individuals in a community forum.

## Join a club

An individual that wishes to either make friends or become a more sociable person should join a club or social organization. A club is usually formed by a group of individuals who may share similar interests, goals, or personal experiences. The main concept of a club or social organization is to allow individuals the opportunity to socialize and participate in specific subject activities with other individuals. There are so many different clubs which come in various different forms. Here are some of following sources for finding a club or social organization:

## Search Engine on the Internet

The internet is the greatest resource for finding and searching information on almost anything in the world. It is a great source for reading the latest news, listening to music, playing online games, and socializing with people all around the world. This source is great for searching for groups or organizations to join and participate in. A group or organization can be found on the internet through searching keywords on various search engines. The search engines will provide you with web sites related to your key words. There are various forms of web sites that allow you to participate in social events. The internet offers community boards that may be located on interest based web sites. A community board is usually established on a web site where there is a focus theme. An example of a focus theme would include a video games community board. This video games community board would allow anyone who has an interest in video games the opportunity to express their ideas and emotions. The community boards are usually run by moderators who are responsible for monitoring the activities in a community board. Most of the moderators and members of the community board participate in various debates and provide information to other members. Some of the information that is posted in the community board may include social events. The social events are established at a physical location such as a public entertainment center or someone's house. These events allow members of a community board to participate in activities that reflect their personal internet. A video games community board event may include a video games competition. The community boards are usually updated on a specific time basis such as daily, weekly, or monthly. You should be able to find any community board that will accommodate your interest. Some people may even choose to create their own community board if they fail to locate a community board that meets their personal interest. The community board allows you to connect and socialize with people all around the world.

## Looking through your local newspaper

The local newspaper is filled with local stories and advertisements. The advertisements generally represent businesses and events that may occur in the local area. You can search the classified section to find information on local organizations or social events. Most of the social event advertisements will display a date, time, and location of an event. The local organization advertisements may display contact information on how to join an organization. There are stories in the local newspaper that may focus on promoting a social event or organization. You can stay updated on local events by purchasing a newspaper either on a daily or weekly basis.

## Search for local advertisements or banners in your town.

Some organizations may advertisement their interest or social events to the public by displaying flyers in the local area. You can find advertisements in local restaurants, retail stores, public library, and other public places. Most libraries carry an events bulletin board which allows the public to display advertisements for local social clubs and events.

A social club can offer a variety of opportunities to the public. You get a chance of socializing with other people that may share the same interest as you. A theme focused social event allows you to build up confidence and social experience. You can increase your ability to express your own opinions and ideas with people that share the same interest. A club or social event is a great way for practicing your social skills.

# <u>Chapter Six</u>

# I need a job

- How do I get a job?

- How to conduct a job search

- Job Application

- Job Application Online Survey

# Chapter Six

# I need a job

We have to worry about the little daily conflicts such as deciding what to eat or what to wear. The conflict that most of our society worries about relates to anything career related. Our society forces us to work for a living. You cannot have food or clothes without money. The only thing that gives us money and the ability to survive in our society is a stable career. A stable career is a job that provides financial security for an individual. There are several different steps to take in building and achieving a stable career.

## How do I get a job?

This is one of the most common questions that are asked by people who either do not currently have a job or have difficulties of attaining employment. The first step in answering this question involves building a person's determination and motivation. A person must have a desire to get a job and work for someone. You must be able to sacrifice your personal time to work under someone's company. A potential employee is usually encouraged to develop their own ways of motivating themselves in achieving goals at the work place. There is no one that can force you to get a job and work except for yourself. You as the individual must develop your own pathway in achieving financial success.

The second step after building and confirming your determination of getting a job would include brainstorming your job interest. It would be difficult to work in an environment in which you have absolutely no interest in. A person who wishes to look for a job must determine what career they would prefer to work in. A career preference can be considered a huge influence in finding a job that is suitable to a person's interest. You can increase your ability and motivation to work in an environment that may meet your personal interest.

Some people prefer to work in an environment that matches their own personal interest. An interesting work environment increases a person's ability to learn more about their career. Here is an example of associating an interest with an occupation:

### *Example 1*

James is a college baseball player who wishes to either become a pro baseball player or enter into a baseball related career. He ends up graduating college without signing any professional baseball contracts. The desire to be involved in a baseball environment motivated him to pursue a career in baseball. James used his personal knowledge of baseball and his degree in sports management to pursue a career in managing baseball related events. He was hired after graduation by a pro baseball team to manage sports promotions and sales. James was able to use his personal interest and pursue a career in which he will be more comfortable in learning and becoming successful.

The above example displayed the success of associating a personal interest with a career. You can begin to the next step after determining your personal job interest. The third step after developing ideas on what career to pursue would include taking the initiative of searching for a job. Some people may find it difficult to look for a job, but sometimes it may be one of the easiest tasks to do in your life. There are many different sources to look through when engaging the activity of a job search. Here are the following sources to use when conducting a job search:

## The local newspaper

The local newspaper is a great source to use in finding jobs in the local surrounding areas. The job postings are usually located in the employment section of your local newspaper. You would be able to find contact information, job title, and even the job description. Some employers may display the required hours and pay rate that they are willing to offer.

There are many advantages of using the local newspaper as a job searching resource. The most important advantage is the opportunity to compare the similarities and differences between each individual job posting. The ability to compare and contrast allows you as the potential candidate to view and analyze your options. Some companies may offer more opportunities compared to other jobs. An example of an opportunity would include a company based tuition reimbursement plan. Some companies may and may not offer this kind of opportunity. The employment section in a newspaper provides job seekers with the opportunity to find a job that is most compatible to a person's personal preferences. You would be able to analyze the negatives or disadvantages between one company and another. Here is an example of analyzing an employment section, comparing job postings, and selecting the best job to apply for:

*Example 2*

### *The Jimmy Chung Times*
## EMPLOYMENT SECTION 2007

1) Sales Associate Position: Must be able to lift 20 lbs, work 40 hours weekly, and work in a fast paced environment. Please contact Mr. Jones at 800-000-0000 if you are interested.

2) We currently have a Cashier position open. Qualifications: previous cashier experience and must be able to work a minimum of 30 hours weekly. Pay rate: 8 dollars an hour. Please email us at <u>employment@joespizzaemployment.com</u> for more information about this position.

3) Tire changer position is available! No experience necessary. Please call us at 800-000-000 to set up an interview.

4) Store Manager Position: Our Company is seeking any individual who has 2-5 years of retail management experience. We offer health insurance, 401k plan, tuition reimbursement, and a sign on bonus of $1000. You will be required to work 40+ hours a week with an annual salary of $60k per year.

5) Joe's General Retail Store is looking for a new Store Manager. We are offering candidates with a 40 hour week, 20 dollars per hour, benefits, tuition reimbursement, and pay vacation. Requirements: Must have 3-5 years of retail management experience and able to lead a team

of up to 30 employees.  You can contact Joe at 800-000-000 to set up an interview.

6) Restaurant Manager position is available at The Green Kiwi Shoppe. Job Requirements: Must be willing to work 55+ hours on an annual salary of 30k per year.

7) Sean's Discount Automotive has a car sales associate position open to only qualified candidates. Job requirements: All candidates must have at least 2 years of sales experience and a driver's license. We offer a great commission based compensation program. Please feel free to call us at 800-000-000 or email us at hrm anagement@seansdiscountautomotive for more information.

*Example 2 Analysis*

The 7 examples all displayed information to attract potential candidates. Every example provided a phone number or email address to allow candidates the ability to contact the employers. The contact information also allows candidates to attain more information about the companies and the chance to schedule an interview.  Most companies in today's society will include a phone number and email to increase the chances of attracting potential company employees.

The examples all contained information on required work hours except for examples two and seven. It is always important to find out how many hours does an employer require you to work. You want to find the company that has the most reasonable work hours to accommodate your personal life. Some people prefer to work part time hours where they may use the rest of their time besides work to study in school or take care of their personal life. Some people prefer to work full time to reach a financial goal or monthly bills.

The majority of the job postings in this example included a pay rate. An employer can pay you through a variety of payment methods. Most companies pay their employees by the hour. The choice of choosing to be pay by the hour has its advantages and disadvantages. The advantage of getting paid by the hour would include overtime pay and the ability to work less hours. Every employee who works and gets paid by the hour must be compensated for any overtime hours worked. The disadvantage of getting paid by the hour would include losing money on sick days. Some companies may not pay you for taking a day off of work. The third payment method that was offered in the example included a commission based position. There are advantages and disadvantages of taking a commission based job. The advantage of a commission based position would generally include the opportunity to make unlimited amount of money. The more sales and transactions that you complete will gain you more money. The disadvantage of taking a commission based position would include a company's requirement of encouraging each employee to work a specific minimum set of hours. You may work for a specific set of hours and still not get paid unless you were able to make a sale. There is a chance to make a great amount of money and there is chance of making no money in a commissioned based position. This compensation type is only encouraged for individuals who are aggressive at selling products and services. A person decides to work in a commission based environment is usually required to have patience and determination. You must be able to encourage and motivate yourself to make a sale and maintain your job. Some companies will rather terminate you than invest their time and money into retraining you to become a profit making salesperson.

Most of the job postings in this example included an employment requirement. An employer usually establishes an employment requirement to increase the chances of interviewing a well qualified prospect. The majority of the employment requirements included a specific amount of experience. Most employers want a candidate who has experience in the same industry. An experience candidate is more likely to be successful than a candidate with absolutely no experience.

There are several ways to select the best potential job for you to pursue. Here are some of the questions that you must answer when analyzing any job postings:

1) Does the potential job meet my personal interest?

2) Do I have enough experience to perform well in this job?

3) Do I have enough experience to meet the requirements?

4) How many hours do I really want to work on a daily and weekly basis?

5) How much money do I deserve?

6) How do I want to get paid? (hourly, salaried, or commission)

7) Do I need a job with tuition reimbursement?

8) Are benefits important to me?

The job offer that meets your answers to these questions is considered to be more compatible than the rest of the job offers. You should compare the advantages and disadvantages between all the job offers that meet your interest. You can begin calling or contacting the potential employers for an interview after analyzing your choices.

## Job posting web sites

The internet is filled with many different web sites that focus on employment. Some web sites will give you advice on how to get a job. There are even web sites that provide national and state statistics concerning average salaries in a specific job position or industry. The most helpful web sites that will assist you in getting a job are the ones that provide job postings. There are web sites that carry an internal search engine which will allow you to search the job of your choice through selecting various features. Some of these various features may include selecting a type of industry, job position, job location, date of job posting, and an employer's name. Most employers in the modern day prefer to use well known employment sites to recruit new employees into their company. The employers generally display contact information, job title, job description, and basic company requirements.

Every potential candidate or employment seeker may use the employment web sites to compare wages, types of jobs, and benefits between various companies. The job seeker is given the opportunity to choose the best employer that will accommodate their interest. The employment web site also works the other way around where job seekers get the opportunity to post their resumes. An employer can search the employment web site by completing a set of requirements for the internal search engine to perform a search. The employer has the opportunity to find candidates that meet their experience and education requirements. The employment web site provides the employer with a list of candidates to be evaluated. This method saves time for the company recruiter since he or she may be able to eliminate unnecessary interviews. The employer has the chance to interview only the best candidates available out of a specific list.

The job postings on a web site are generally opened to the public to view. Most employers allow potential candidates to directly apply through an employment web site. Some employers prefer candidates to click on a link within the employment web site, which directs them into the employer's company web site.

## Company web sites

Every employer has their own employment requirements. Some employers may require you to simply fill out an application form. There are other employers who practice strict hiring practices to increase their chances of finding the most hardworking professional that they can hire. Some of the strict hiring practices may require all applicants to fill out an online application on a company's web site. The online application may contain a survey or a theme related test to determine whether a candidate to suitable for an interview. Some of these online application tests are used to evaluate a person's ability to perform certain duties. Here is an example of what an online application test may look like:

*Example 3*

# Mr. Average Joe's Sports Shop Online
## Application Survey

### Company Scenario Section 1

1) What would you if you witness a fellow employee stealing from the store's cash register?

   a) Tell the employee to stop stealing.
   b) Call the local authorities.
   c) Call the store manager.
   d) Ignore the employee and continue performing your own duties.

2) You are already providing assistance to a customer where another customer approaches you with a request for assistance. What would you do in this situation?

   a) Call another employee to assist the second customer.
   b) Call the manager to assist the second customer.
   c) Tell the second customer that he or she should wait until you are finished with the first customer.
   d) Tell the second customer that you are currently busy.

3) A customer tells you that the price on the cash register does not match the price sign. What would you do in this situation?

   a) Tell the customer that the price on the cash register is the correct price.
   b) Tell the customer that he or she is wrong.

    c) Call an available associate to confirm a price check.

    d) Call the store manager to confirm a price check.

4) A customer takes a piece of store merchandise and runs out of the store. What would you do in this situation?

    a) Chase after the customer.

    b) Tell the customer to stop.

    c) Notify the store security team.

    d) Notify the local authorities.

5) A customer becomes furious and starts yelling at you. What should you do in this situation?

    a) Tell the customer to get out of the store.

    b) Try to analyze the customer's problem.

    c) Call a nearby manager for assistance.

    d) Call another associate for assistance.

## Company Psychological Section 2

6) Do you consider yourself to be a hard worker?

    a) I strongly agree.

    b) I agree.

    c) I don't know.

    d) I disagree.

    e) I strongly disagree.

7) How do you feel about working in a fast paced environment?

    a) I strongly agree.

    b) I agree.

    c) I don't know.
    d) I disagree.
    e) I strongly disagree.

8) Do you consider yourself to be a confident person?

    a) I strongly agree.
    b) I agree.
    c) I don't know.
    d) I disagree.
    e) I strongly disagree.

9) Are you willing to follow orders from a team of managers?

    a) I strongly disagree.
    b) I disagree.
    c) I don't know.
    d) I agree.
    e) I strongly agree.

10) Are you the kind of employee that may call out once or twice each month?

    a) I strongly disagree.
    b) I disagree.
    c) I don't know.
    d) I agree.
    e) I strongly agree.

11) Do you consider yourself to be a leader or take charge type?

    a) I strongly agree.
    b) I agree.

c) I don't know.
d) I disagree.
e) I strongly disagree.

12) Do you consider yourself to be a happy person?

    a) I strongly disagree.
    b) I disagree.
    c) I don't know.
    d) I agree.
    e) I strongly agree.

13) Do other people view you as a hardworking person?

    a) I strongly agree.
    b) I agree.
    c) I don't know.
    d) I disagree.
    e) I strongly disagree.

14) Do other people view you as a happy outgoing person?

    a) I strongly disagree.
    b) I disagree.
    c) I don't know.
    d) I agree.
    e) I strongly agree.

15) Do you consider yourself to be an optimistic person?

    a) I strongly agree.
    b) I agree.
    c) I don't know.
    d) I disagree.
    e) I strongly disagree.

16) Do other people consider you to be an optimistic person?

    a) I strongly agree.
    b) I agree.
    c) I don't know.
    d) I disagree.
    e) I strongly disagree.

17) Are you currently depressed?

    a) I strongly agree.
    b) I agree.
    c) I don't know.
    d) I disagree.
    e) I strongly disagree.

18) Are you currently satisfied with your life?

    a) I strongly disagree.
    b) I disagree.
    c) I don't know.
    d) I agree.
    e) I strongly agree.

19) Do you consider yourself to be a friendly person?

    a) I strongly agree.
    b) I agree.
    c) I don't know.
    d) I disagree.
    e) I strongly disagree.

20) Do you enjoy working with other people?

       a)  I strongly agree.
       b)  I agree.
       c)  I don't know.
       d)  I disagree.
       e)  I strongly disagree.

21) Do you consider yourself to be an angry person?

       a)  I strongly agree.
       b)  I agree.
       c)  I don't know.
       d)  I disagree.
       e)  I strongly disagree.

22) Do other people consider you to be an angry person?

       a)  I strongly agree.
       b)  I agree.
       c)  I don't know.
       d)  I disagree.
       e)  I strongly disagree.

23) Do you enjoy the company of other people?

       a)  I strongly agree.
       b)  I agree.
       c)  I don't know.
       d)  I disagree.
       e)  I strongly disagree.

24) How do you feel about taking merchandise from the store?

a) I strongly agree.
b) I agree.
c) I don't know.
d) I disagree.
e) I strongly disagree.

25) Do you care about another person's emotional feelings?

a) I strongly agree.
b) I agree.
c) I don't know.
d) I disagree.
e) I strongly disagree.

26) Do you consider yourself to be a professional type of person?

a) I strongly disagree.
b) I disagree.
c) I don't know.
d) I agree.
e) I strongly agree.

27) Do you consider yourself to be a well relaxed person?
a) I strongly agree.
b) I agree.
c) I don't know.
d) I disagree.
e) I strongly disagree.

28) Do you consider yourself to be a stressful person?

a) I strongly agree.
b) I agree.
c) I don't know.

d) I disagree.

e) I strongly disagree.

29) Are you usually calm when it comes to any tough or difficult situation?

a) I strongly agree.

b) I agree.

c) I don't know.

d) I disagree.

e) I strongly disagree.

30) Do you consider yourself to be a sociable person?

a) I strongly disagree.

b) I disagree.

c) I don't know.

d) I agree.

e) I strongly agree.

31) Do other people consider you to be a stressful person?

a) I strongly agree.

b) I agree.

c) I don't know.

d) I disagree.

e) I strongly disagree.

32) Do you consider yourself to be a person with the ability to create bright new ideas?

a) I strongly agree.

b) I agree.

c) I don't know.

d) I disagree.

e) I strongly disagree.

33) Do you like working in situations where a time limit is established?

    a) I strongly agree.
    b) I agree.
    c) I don't know.
    d) I disagree.
    e) I strongly disagree.

34) Do you like working in a slow paced environment?

    a) I strongly agree.
    b) I agree.
    c) I don't know.
    d) I disagree.
    e) I strongly disagree.

35) Do other people consider you to be a sociable person?

    a) I strongly disagree.
    b) I disagree.
    c) I don't know.
    d) I agree.
    e) I strongly agree.

36) Are you the type of person that prefers to do things by the book?

    a) I strongly agree.
    b) I agree.
    c) I don't know.
    d) I disagree.
    e) I strongly disagree.

37) Do you become stressed out when you encounter a tough situation?

   a) I strongly agree.
   b) I agree.
   c) I don't know.
   d) I disagree.
   e) I strongly disagree.

38) Do other people view you as a professional type of person?

   a) I strongly agree.
   b) I agree.
   c) I don't know.
   d) I disagree.
   e) I strongly disagree.

39) Are you dedicated to the work that you are responsible for?

   a) I strongly disagree.
   b) I disagree.
   c) I don't know.
   d) I agree.
   e) I strongly agree.

40) Do other people consider you to be a responsible person?

   a) I strongly disagree.
   b) I disagree.
   c) I don't know.
   d) I agree.
   e) I strongly agree.

41) Are you likely to defend yourself in a verbal argument?

    a) I strongly disagree.
    b) I disagree.
    c) I don't know.
    d) I agree.
    e) I strongly agree.

42) Do other people respect you as a person?

    a) I strongly disagree.
    b) I disagree.
    c) I don't know.
    d) I agree.
    e) I strongly agree.

43) Would other people consider you to be a dependable person?

    a) I strongly disagree.
    b) I disagree.
    c) I don't know.
    d) I agree.
    e) I strongly agree.

44) Do you take time to think before making a decision?

    a) I strongly agree.
    b) I agree.
    c) I don't know.
    d) I disagree.
    e) I strongly disagree.

45) Are you confident with your decision making skills?

a) I strongly agree.
b) I agree.
c) I don't know.
d) I disagree.
e) I strongly disagree.

46) Do you consider yourself to be a rebellious type of person?

a) I strongly agree.
b) I agree.
c) I don't know.
d) I disagree.
e) I strongly disagree.

47) Do you have any problems with taking orders from the management team?

a) I strongly agree.
b) I agree.
c) I don't know.
d) I disagree.
e) I strongly disagree.

48) Are you the type of person that can be easily distracted?

a) I strongly agree.
b) I agree.
c) I don't know.
d) I disagree.
e) I strongly disagree.

49) Do you consider yourself to be a multitask type of person?

   a) I strongly agree.
   b) I agree.
   c) I don't know.
   d) I disagree.
   e) I strongly disagree.

50) Do you believe your future managers will consider you to be an excellent worker?

   a) I strongly agree.
   b) I agree.
   c) I don't know.
   d) I disagree.
   e) I strongly disagree.

# Mr. Average Joe's Sports Shop Online
## Application Survey Scoring System

| Total Points | Result |
|---|---|
| 0-10pts | Bad |
| 11-20pts | Bad |
| 21-30pts | Average |
| 31-40pts | Good |
| 41-50pts | Excellent |

This job application survey is used by many companies today to evaluate and determine whether a candidate is eligible for an interview. Every human resource or general manager would prefer to avoid interviewing nonqualified candidates. This job application online survey has the potential and ability to save a great amount of time and money for many companies. A manager can spend more time on selling products or fulfilling their required duties instead of spending a great amount of time on interviewing unnecessary candidates. The first part of this example evaluated the candidate's personal working ethics. It is important to evaluate what a potential candidate would do in specific situations. This example focused on a retail store where certain factors are required to ensure excellent performance. The employees in a retail store or business environment are usually required to be outgoing, assertive, organized, and contain the ability to practice excellent customer service. The customer is usually considered the most important person in a business. A customer is the reason why a business stays in the competitive business market. You cannot have a business without the presence of a customer.

The second part of the job application online survey involves testing a candidate's personality and personal beliefs. Every question is created to attract the personality traits of a person. This online survey is use for evaluating how the candidate views themselves and people around them. You may have noticed that the majority of the questions seem similar to each other. Most businesses tend to repeat their questions to evaluate a candidate's honesty and whether their answers were accurate. This method of placing similar or repeated questions increases the chance of receiving the most accurate results. You may have noticed that some of the answers were switched around. The answer switching method is used to prevent and discourage applicants from selecting the same answer in a repetitive fashion.

Every job application online survey has a scoring system. The scoring system evaluates an individual based on their answers during the survey. The recruiter or manager will view the results to verify whether a candidate should be called in for an interview. You don't have to worry about getting a perfect score, but you will need to get a good score. A good score can still get you employed into a company, but a terrible score will immediately eliminate you from receiving an interview. You may get the same scores as another person and still get an interview. The interview determines whether you can be hired or not. You have to remember that an online application survey does not determine whether you will be hired by a company or not. Here is an example of what may happen when manager receives the final survey scores from multiple potential candidates:

# Mr. Average Joe's Sports Shop Online
## Application Survey Final Scores Recruitment Management

| Total Points | Result | Name | Interview |
|---|---|---|---|
| 43 | Excellent | Jimmy | Yes |
| 40 | Good | Kelly | Yes |
| 31 | Good | Brian | Yes |
| 35 | Good | Robert | Yes |
| 12 | Bad | Kevin | No |
| 43 | Excellent | Sarah | Yes |

The job application online survey varies from one company to another. Some companies will require you to fill out an online test where other companies may just accept you application. This example should be used as a reference or an idea of what to expect when you plan on applying for a job. You must always remember read each question and answer carefully to avoid producing inaccurate results. The worst outcome from creating inaccurate results may include not getting employed.

# Chapter Seven

# Presenting yourself to the Employer

- Developing a cover letter.
- State your address.
- State your date.
- Name and address of employer.
- Place a greeting.
- Cover Letter Introduction.
- Cover Letter Body Paragraph.
- Cover Letter Conclusion.
- Closing your cover letter.

# Chapter Seven

# Presenting a cover letter to the Employer

There are many different steps to take in getting a job. You have to prepare yourself before walking into your future employer's office. It is important to remember that you may have to compete with various candidates for a position. Everyone has their own unique experiences, level of education, and personalities. The employer will only pick the best individual out of the applicant pool. You are responsible for presenting yourself to the employer as one of the best individuals out of the applicant pool. Most employers will judge you as a person and future employee during an interview process. We previously discuss the importance of dominating the application and the application surveys. The next step is to support your application with your personal and past information.

### Developing a cover letter

The cover letter is a page that is written to the company that you wish to apply to. This letter reflects a summary of your education, personality, and previous employment highlights. You only list previous achievements that are appropriate to the company that you wish to become apart of. The goal of this letter is an excellent way for you to introduce yourself to the employer. The employer becomes notified that you are interested in their company. This is a great chance to establish communications and relationship. The cover letter will allow the employer to learn something about you before any managers decide to call you for an interview. The cover letter should include the following steps:

## State your address

You should always state your address on the very top corner of the cover letter. The employer will use your address to contact you for an interview or further employment processing. The personal address should include your mailing address and a way for the employer to contact you. The two most common contact methods include a phone number and email address. Here is an example of how your mailing address should look like on the cover letter (top left corner of the cover letter):

**51 Your Address Rd**
**My town, NY 10000**
(800) 000-0000

## State the date

The date is usually established under your address, but on the right corner of the cover letter. The right corner allows the employer to easily access the date of when the cover letter was submitted. Some employers will throw out a cover letter if there is no date present. A non-dated cover letter will discourage an employer from contacting you since they do not know the submission date of the cover letter. You should always remember to place the correct date when submitting your cover letter. Here is an example of a cover letter date (below address, top right corner):

May 21st, 2007

## Name and Address of Employer

The next step after stating your date involves establishing the name and address of your employer. You want to make sure that the cover letter is sent to the correct recipient. The cover letter looks more personal when you add a name and address. The addition of a name and address will tell the employer that you spent some personal time to research their contact information. Most employers will appreciate a personal cover letter and acknowledge you for having a strong interest to work in their company. It is important to remember that the employer's personal name, company name, and address are displayed below the date. Here is an example of a proper name and address (below date, left side of the cover letter):

**Mr. John Manage**
**John's Sporting Goods**
**19 Sporting Goods Rd**
**Rockland, NY 10000**

### Place a greeting

The address of the employer should be followed by a greeting. The greeting is located a single or two lines under the employer's address on the left side of the cover letter. Here is an example:

Dear Mr. John Good,

### Cover Letter Introduction

The introduction is the most important part of the cover letter. You will use this section to introduce yourself as an interested candidate. This section should include your name and why are interested in working for the employer. You should include a detail explanation of why you want to work for a specific employer. The introduction should include the position that you wish to apply for. The employer will acknowledge your interest and keep your resume in mind. Here is an example of a cover letter introduction (located a few lines under the greeting):

## *Cover Letter Introduction Example*

My name is Average Joe and I would be interested in working for your company. John's Sporting Goods provides many job opportunities where I would like to become an employee. This company is the perfect place for me to grow and develop into a successful business person. I wish to grow with your company by gaining a position as a Sales Manager. The Sales Manager position contains responsibilities and duties that I'm very familiar with. I would enjoy starting as a Sales Manager with hopes to grow and climb the company's management ladder.

## Cover Letter Body Paragraph

This section will be used to describe your past experience. You do not need to list all your achievements or past employers since your resume will contain all your employment information. The body paragraph of the cover letter should only contain the main highlights of your past employment, education history, and personal experiences. Here is an example of a cover letter body paragraph (located a single line under the introduction paragraph):

## Cover Letter Body Paragraph Example

My career goal of attaining a Sales Manager position in your company can be supported with my previous career history. I believe your company will benefit from my five years of experience as a former Sales Manager at Bobby's Sporting Goods. Most of my responsibilities included basic store accounting, tracking inventory, store marketing, recruiting, creating weekly work schedules, and managing a team of 50 employees. My latest education achievement includes the completion of a four year Bachelors of Science degree in Business Management from the University of Business Management. The knowledge that I acquired from the degree program would be used to increase your sales and manage a successful team. I believe I have the ability to learn and apply my previous experience with a goal of improving your business.

## Cover Letter Conclusion

The conclusion would close the cover letter with a closing statement. It should include a summary of why you want to work for the employer. The conclusion will be the last paragraph that the recruiting or hiring manager will read. This section is your last chance to leave an impression that the employer will be forced to remember your name. You may include something about your personality. Some managers are interested to find out what kind of person you are. An outgoing and professional personality may increase your chances of landing a new job. Here is an example of a Cover Letter Conclusion (located a single line under the cover letter body paragraph):

## Cover Letter Conclusion Example

Most of my previous managers and colleagues have classified me as an assertive and professional person. I believe my organizational and leadership skills will give your company an advantage in competing with your competitors. I'm always willing to learn new materials and techniques. The value of learning something new can improve your chances of gaining success. I would be honored to become employed and learn from your company's unique methods. I look forward to hearing from you soon. Thank you for your time and have a nice day.

## Closing your Cover Letter

This section is your opportunity to successfully close your cover letter. You do not need to write anything more than the word sincerely and your name. This part of the cover letter is the same as writing any letter. You should include sincerely just a few lines below your conclusion paragraph. The next part is to skip a few lines and write your full name. You may place a signature between the words sincerely and your name. A signature is not necessary where it is only up to the applicant to decide. Here is an example of how to close your cover letter (located a few lines under the cover letter conclusion paragraph):

*Closing your Cover Letter Example*

Sincerely,

(Space for signature)

Average Joe

We discussed how to write a cover letter by displaying an example of each part. It is important to remember to summarize only the strong points of your resume. The cover letter only acts as a summary of your resume. You should not establish all your past career and education achievements in the cover letter. The cover letter should be kept short to avoid decreasing your employer's interest. Here is a full example of how a cover letter may look like:

*Cover Letter Full Example*

51 Your Address Rd
My town, NY 10000
(800) 000-0000

May 21st, 2007

Mr. John Manage
John's Sporting Goods
19 Sporting Goods Rd
Rockland, NY 10000

Dear Average Joe,

My name is Average Joe and I would be interested in working for your company. John's Sporting Goods provides many job opportunities where I would like to become an employee. This company is the perfect place for me to grow and develop into a successful business person. I wish to grow with your company by gaining a position as a Sales Manager. The Sales Manager position contains responsibilities and duties that I'm very familiar with. I would enjoy starting as a Sales Manager with hopes to grow and climb the company's management ladder.

My career goal of attaining a Sales Manager position in your company can be supported with my previous career history. I believe your company will benefit from my five years of experience as a former Sales Manager at Bobby's Sporting Goods. Most of my responsibilities included basic store accounting, tracking inventory, store marketing, recruiting, creating weekly work schedules, and managing a team of 50 employees. My latest education achievement includes the completion of a four year Bachelors of Science degree in Business Management from the University of Business Management. The knowledge that I acquired from the degree program would be used to increase your sales and manage a successful team. I believe I have the ability to learn and apply my previous experience with a goal of improving your business.

Most of my previous managers and colleagues have classified me as an assertive and professional person. I believe my organizational and leadership skills will give your company an advantage in competing with your competitors. I'm always willing to learn new materials and techniques. The value of learning something new can improve your chances of gaining success. I would be honored to become employed and learn from your company's unique methods. I look forward to hearing from you soon. Thank you for your time and have a nice day.

Sincerely,


Average Joe

# Chapter Eight

# Getting attention from the Employer

- Developing a resume.
- Proper attire.
- How to conquer your interview.
- Building experience.
- How do I get a promotion?

# Chapter Eight

# Getting attention from the Employer

The employer or a manager is the most important person to impress in your career. This individual is responsible for giving you a job or promoting you into a higher position. The first step of getting the employer's attention is to develop a resume.

## Developing a resume

The next step is to support your information on the cover letter with a detailed resume. A resume contains your past employment and educational history. The employer will mostly focus on evaluating your resume to determine eligibility for an interview. There are many different sections of a resume. We will break down each section, so that you will be able to effectively create and present a strong resume. You have to remember that the contents in the resume depend on your personal abilities and experience. It is encouraged to avoid placing false information in your resume. The actions of placing false information may lead you to fail in the interview process or receive a termination notice from your employer. The contents of the resume represent your skills as a professional and an individual. The employer will hire you based on the information presented in your resume. You would be expected to use your knowledge and experience in the work place. There is absolutely no reason for you to create and display false information on your resume. Most recruiting managers will eventually detect whether you are telling the truth or not.

The resume is consisted of multiple sections where each one will outline your experience. The sections of a resume are a representation of who you are as a professional. Here is a step by step example of how to create an effective resume:

## State the date

The date of when the resume was create and submitted should be placed on the upper right corner of the resume. The employer would use the date to determine the time period of when your resume was last submitted. The date is the same format as your cover letter (top right corner).

*State the date example*

May 21st, 2007

## State your name, address, contact information

This information will be used by the employer or interviewer to contact you with further information concerning your employment. You should always state your full name with your physical and mailing address. The contact information should be placed below the mailing address. The full name should be in bold to indicate and remind the employer that the resume belongs to you. It is recommended to provide more than one contact source. You may leave one or two email addresses, one home phone number, and a cellular number if you have a cell phone. The multiple communication resources would allow the employer to easily reach you. Here is an example of how your contact information should be formatted (skip one line below date, established on left side):

*Contact Information example*

**Jimmy Chung**
345 Conflict Rd

Management, NY 10000
Home Phone: (800) 000-0000
Cell Phone: 1-800-000 -0000Email: <u>info@jimmychung.</u>
<u>com</u>

## Preference

Some people have a preference when it comes to giving out contact information. You may state specific hours that you are available to communicate whether it's on the phone or on the internet. The employer can avoid calling you on times when you are busy. You should take advantage of listing a contact preference if you prefer one contact source over another. Some people prefer to send electronic resumes rather than contacting a manager by phone. Here is an example of a communication preference (skip a line below the contact information, left side of the resume).

*Preference example*
**Preference:** I prefer to be contacted by my email address.

## Objective

The objective describes your desired position or field of interest. The employer can have a better idea of what position to offer you by evaluating your objective. You may have a greater chance of getting a specific position if you list your main objective. Here is an example of an objective (skip a line, establish under preferences, left side of resume):

## *Objective example*

**Objective:** To find an entry level job/internship into regional sales/human resources/management.

## Education

Some employers may require all candidates to meet their education requirement. You can provide the employer with your education background by listing your previous educational institute. If you are currently in school then you may list your year of graduation. Some employers will hire you even if you haven't completed your degree or certificate program. Here is an example of education outline (skip one line, establish on left side below objective):

### *Education example*

**Education:** University of Management, Name of City, New York.

YOG: 2006, Associates in Business Degree
YOG: 2008, Bachelors in Business Management: Human Resources Management Degree

## Academic Achievement

The academic achievement section can put on top of your competitors. Some employers will appreciate your hard work in the academic environment. Most managers admire above average students where they prefer to hire the most intelligent and hard working individuals. Here is an example of the Academic Achievement section (skip a line, located on left side, below education):

### *Academic Achievement example*

**Academic Achievement:** Received a four year Student Leadership Scholarship (University of Management). Recognized for high achievement in the first two semesters at the University of Management.

## Special Skills

The special skills section allows you as an individual to display your unique talents. This section is generally used for listing your ability to speak, write, or read in a specific language. Most employers will hire multilingual candidates since they have the ability to communicate with a variety of customers. A multilingual employee may boost sales for a company by giving customers the opportunity to communicate. Here is an example of the Special Skills section (skip a line, establish on left side under academic achievement):

*Special Skills example*

**Special Skills**: Speaks English and Chinese

## Applied Skills

The applied skills section allows you as the individual to list your useful skills. This section is a great opportunity to show the employer the skills that you have acquired in the past. These skills may include you ability to use a specific software or type of machinery. Here is an example of a applied skills section (skip a line, left side, established under special skills):

*Applied Skills example*

**Applied Skills**: Personal Computer hardware, Internet literate, basic knowledge of Local Area Network (LAN), Office Software 2003 + 2004, and basic knowledge of website building.

## Work Experience

Most employers will require you to have previous work experience. You can start at an entry level position if you do not have any work experience. This section should include all your previous employment information. The list of your previous companies should be stated in a specific chronological style. The most previous employment company should be listed first, which should be followed with your second previous company. The work experience section should include your previous employer's name, city, state, job title, job description, employee recognition, and the time period between getting hired and being terminated. The interviewer will be interested in evaluating how long you stayed at your previous jobs and how many jobs did you have in the past few years. The employer will evaluate your previous job titles and descriptions to see if you are experience enough to be employed. Here is an example of the work experience section (skip a line, left side, established under applied skills).

Work Experience example

**Work Experience:**

2005 – 2006, Joe's Sporting Goods, Hartford,
Connecticut.
Store Manager: Managed 30 employees, responsible for store accounting, marketing displays, and customer service. *Excellence Award* for the Month of March 2006.

2004- 2005, University of Management, Orange City, New York. Information Desk Monitor: Duties included assigning recreational equipment, organizing the UM student center lounge, and inform visitors with directions to events within the center.

2003 – 2004, Big Red Management Corporation,
Orangetown, New York.
Department Manager: Duties included store marketing, selling merchandise, managing 10 employees, and updating department inventory.

**Extracurricular**

Some employers will use the extracurricular section to analyze your personality. Most employers want to know who you are before they decide to hire you. You may be able to impress your interviewer if you happen to share a common interest with them. A great amount of extracurricular activities would show the employer that you are an active and multi-task person. Some jobs will require all candidates to be able to handle a fast paced and multitask based environment. Here is an example of the extracurricular section (skip a line, established on left side under work experience):

*Extracurricular example*

**Extracurricular:**

2004 – 2005, UM Tennis Club and UM National
          Leaders Club.

2003, Town of Waternut Business Club (Vice President).

2000 – 2003, Town of Waternut Men's Volleyball League
          (Team Captain).

**References**

Most employers will require you to provide them with more than one reference. It is recommended to list at least two references. The references can be your personal friends, coworkers, and your previous managers. You should always list your relationship to your reference and their phone number. Most employers prefer to speak with your references on the phone. You should not provide an email address since the employer will not be able to determine whether the email belongs to you or the actual reference. Some people do not know their immediate references, so they take the approach of placing the words "available upon request". The employer will eventually just ask you for a reference at a later time if you do not provide one immediately.

*Reference examples*

**References:**

Sean Johnson (personal friend), 800-000-000.
Amy Williams (Manager of Big Red Management Corporation), 800-000-000

**Or**

**References:**

Available upon request.


**Full Resume Example**

May 21$^{st}$, 2007

**Jimmy Chung**
345 Conflict Rd
Management, NY 10000
Home Phone: (800) 000-0000
Cell Phone: 1-800-000 -0000
Email: info@jimmychung.com
**Preference:** I prefer to be contacted by my email address.

**Objective:** To find an entry level job/internship into regional sales/human resources/management.
**Education:**
University of Management, Name of City, New York.
YOG: 2006, Associates in Business Degree
YOG: 2008, Bachelors in Business Management: Human Resources Management Degree

**Academic Achievement:**
Received a four year Student Leadership Scholarship (University of Management).

Recognized for high achievement in the first two semesters at the University of Management.

**Special Skills:** Speaks English and Chinese

**Applied Skills**: Personal Computer hardware, Internet literate, basic knowledge of Local Area Network (LAN), Office Software 2003 + 2004, and basic knowledge of website building.

Work Experience:

2005 – 2006, Joe's Sporting Goods, Hartford, Connecticut.

Store Manager: Managed 30 employees, responsible for store accounting, marketing displays, and customer service. *Excellence Award* for the Month of March 2006.

2004- 2005, University of Management, Queens, New York.

Information Desk Monitor: Duties included assigning recreational equipment, organizing the UM student center lounge, and inform visitors with directions to events within the center.

2003 ☒ 2004, Big Red Management Corporation, Orangetown, New York.

Department Manager: Duties included store marketing, selling merchandise, managing 10 employees, and updating department inventory.

Extracurricular:

2004 – 2005, UM Tennis Club and UM National Leaders Club.

2003, Town of Waternut Business Club (Vice President).

2000 – 2003, Town of Waternut Men's Volleyball League (Team Captain).

**References:**

Sean Johnson (personal friend), 800-000-000.

Amy Williams (Manager of Big Red Management Corporation), 800-000-000
**Or**
**References:**
Available upon request.

## Proper attire

Every candidate that decides to go for an interview must dress in a professional and appropriate manner. You have to adjust your appearance to your surroundings especially when it comes to a professional environment. The employer or recruiting manager will judge you on your physical presentation. A professionally dressed person will most likely get a job compared to a person wearing clothes that would fit a party environment. Sometimes it may be best for you as an individual to picture yourself as a manager. I'm sure you would pick a professionally dressed person as opposed to someone who looks like they are ready to party.

A professional style attire will show the employer that you are dedicated to work. Some employers may tell you that a professional appearance may determine whether a person will get hired or not. Most employers will evaluate your personality and determination to work based on your ability to physically present yourself. There are many places where you can purchase professional clothing for a cheap price. You do not have to spend a great amount of money on expensive professional clothes. It is extremely important to dress and make a presentation to the employer in a professional manner.

## How to conquer an interview

Most employers will schedule you for one interview with either a manager or human resource recruiter. Some employers may schedule you for multiple interviews with various managers. Every manager has their own preference in when it comes to hiring employees. Some managers prefer to train an inexperience candidate to become a personal assistant where other managers prefer experience candidates.

Every hiring manager is different, but their main interviewing questions are generally the same. It is your responsibility to be able to answer an interviewer's questions in a professional manner. A well thought and professional answer may increase your ability to get a job. It is true that most people do not know what questions to expect during an interview. Here are some general interview questions that may be asked by the employer:

### General Interview Questions

1) What position are you applying for?

2) Why do you want to work for my company?

3) What kind of skills can you offer my company?

4) What knowledge do you have of my company?

5) When was the last time that you were employed?

6) What company did you previously work for?

7) Why did you leave your last employer?

8) What was your position at your previous company?

9) What was your favorite part while working for your last employer?

10) What was the worst part while working for your last employer?

11) Did you enjoy working with your previous coworkers?

12) Did you enjoy working with your previous managers?

13) How do you feel about working in a fast paced environment?

14) How do you feel about working a slow paced environment?

15) Do you consider yourself a leader or follower?

16) How do you feel about working in a commission based environment?

17) How do you feel about working with others in a team?

18) How do you feel about working full time hours?

19) How do you feel about working part time hours?

20) What was your previous wage or salary?

21) What is your desired wage or salary?

22) When can you start working?

23) Are you willing to commit to a drug test?

24) Do you have any questions for me?

These questions are general interview questions which may be used by various employers. The contents of these questions are used to evaluate the candidate's personality and work ethic. Some of the questions can reveal the past employment experiences of the candidate. A candidate's past performance may be used by employers to create a performance forecast. The performance forecast is basically an estimate of what the candidate may or may not be able to do for the employer.

## Building experience

An employer will most likely hire you if you have multiple years of experience. Some people such as high school students or college graduates may not have any experiences. There are many ways to get experience such as participating in school activities, community service, and an entry level job. An entry level job is usually a basic position where you will be able to train and develop your working skills. This is a great opportunity for you to get your foot into the door. You cannot expect to get a high paid job without any experiences. It will take time, patience, and hours of hard work to gain experience. You should have a better chance of attaining a high level position once you are able to meet an employer's experience requirements.

## How to get a promotion

There are several ways to get a promotion where eligibility requirements vary from one employer to another employer. Some companies may require you to work within the company for a specific time period. Some companies will require you to go through a series of company based training before applying for a promotion. The journey to get a promotion or even competing for a promotion is not an easy task. You will be expected to compete with coworkers and candidates from outside the company. A manager will judge all candidates based on years of experience, company knowledge, position knowledge, special skills, and previous job title. You should always remember that there are many opportunities out in the business or employment market. There are many companies that are willing to give you a position if you current employer fails to promote you. You have to think positive and keep focus on your professional goals.

# Chapter Nine

# Business and Life Conflicts

- Management Conflicts.
- Recruitment Management
- Parenting Conflicts.

# Chapter Nine

# Business Management Conflicts

We must encounter and deal with various conflicts on a daily basis. Some people must deal and solve conflicts involving business related issues. Some conflicts are easy to handle where other conflicts require time and planning to solve. You should always remember that the concepts of critical thinking can improve your chances of producing accurate answers. An accurate solution to a conflict will allow you to produce accurate answers. A great problem solver must evaluate their resources for validity to avoid using fallacy information. This chapter will cover advice on how to handle business management and life related conflicts. You may use the contents of this chapter as a reference to solve your personal, academic, and professional issues.

## Management Conflicts

The management team of a company must deal with conflicts on a daily basis. The conflicts may involve selling a product, serving customers, inventory, marketing, or employee related issues. A manager does not have easy position. Our society has created a stereotypical image of a lazy manager who does nothing, but delegate actions to the employees. The delegation factor is considered a small portion of a manager's duties. Most managers must encounter difficult situations where they must create a decision that can dramatically affect their business. The most common management issue is recruiting and maintaining a full staff of skilled workers. Most companies must deal with the monthly loss of employees. There are many reasons why a company may lose their employees. Some employees may retire where some may have found a better job at another company.

There may be situations where the company is forced to terminate an employee based on company violations, company budget, or poor individual performance.

The loss of employees can decrease the amount of sales and profits for a company. Most major companies are combating the potential fear of losing employees by developing advance hiring methods. Some companies have hired individuals or a third party company that specialize in recruiting, interviewing, and hiring new employees. The professions that specialize in hiring employees may include a Human Resource Manager, Recruitment Manager, and other employment related specialists.

## Recruitment Management

A recruitment manager is responsible for maintaining the number of total employees either for a company or retail store environment. Most companies have established their own staffing and hiring requirements. The requirements may include the minimum and maximum number of employees that are required within a company. There are several ways to track the number of employees in a store. A recruitment manager is usually assisted by department managers who are responsible for managing their own respected departments. The department manager manages the number of employees in their department.

A department manager can assist a recruitment manager by providing updates on whether a department will require more or less employees. The recruitment manager in most companies has the responsibility and authority to either hire or terminate a specific amount of employees. The establishment of a minimum or maximum amount of employees within a department may depend on the business market.

Every season and each month of the year has a major role to play in the employment process. The products and services of a company also play a role in determining whether to hire or terminate employees. Here is an example of how the recruiting requirements may be based on a seasonal period:

## Recruiting based on the Season

### *Example 1*

Jim's Snowboarding shop makes almost all of its sales and profits during the fall and winter season. The fall season allows customers to start purchasing items for the winter. The winter season is where customers tend to contribute the majority of sales and profits for Jim's Snowboarding Shop. The shop sells various sporting goods as addition to their main attraction of snowboarding equipment. The owner of the shop, Jim has established a minimum staffing requirement of 20 employees during the fall and winter season. The maximum is 35 employees during the fall and winter season. Jim has established these staffing numbers to accommodate the great amount of customers who will be willing purchase snowboarding equipment.

In the spring and summer seasons, Jim has to reduce his minimum staff requirement to 10 employees and his maximum to only 15. The reason for the reduced staffing amount is due to their predicted sales in the spring and summer season. The store carries a small portion of various sporting goods compared to their majority of snowboarding products. Jim's Snowboarding Shop will most likely concentrate on their small portion of various sporting goods in the spring and summer season. Jim would lose a great amount of money if he decided to keep the same amount of employees from the fall and winter season. He may not be able to make enough money to cover the salaries of his employees.

## Effective Recruiting

Most recruiting managers have developed their own unique techniques over years of experience. We will break down how to recruit and maintain a well staffed business environment. A recruitment manager must take several steps before they are able to fulfill their employee quota. The first step in effective recruitment is to figure out the number of current employees. The second step involves comparing the number of current employees to your minimum and maximum employee requirements. You have to figure out whether to terminate a specific amount of employees or to hire more employees into your company. If your company needs more employees then you need to search and advertise any available positions.

## Searching for Prospects

Most recruitment managers in the modern day prefer to search for potential employees through job related web sites. The only problem of using a third party web site to recruit candidates would include various fees. The company loses money to a third party web site for posting jobs. Some third party job related web sites attract a great amount of potential candidates, which will increase the chances of finding and hiring a new employee. It is important for a recruitment manager to list the job description, location of the business, and contact information. The applicants will depend on this information to make a decision of whether to apply or not.

Some recruitment managers prefer to participate in local job fairs. This is a great opportunity to conduct an on site interview. You can save time by immediately evaluating any willing applicant. The job fair allows you to create a presentation which may represent your company's products, services, goals, and employment opportunities. The most effective method of attracting applicants is to provide promotional material such as business cards, balloons, pens, and anything that you are authorized to give out for free.

Some companies may establish a career link within their web site that outlines all the current available positions. The lists of various job positions are usually detailed with job descriptions, benefits, and even a starting wage or salary amount. A company web site saves time and money by not sending recruiting managers to job fairs or posting jobs on a third party web site.

## Scheduling an Interview

A recruitment manager will either receive a request from an applicant for an interview or they may call a prospect for an interview. There are several ways to conduct an interview. Here is a variety of interview forms:

### *Phone Interview*

Some managers prefer to conduct an introduction interview before scheduling a face to face interview. A manager in a phone interview would generally ask simple questions involving the candidate's desired wage or position of interest.

### *Individual face to face Interview*

This is the most common interview form. Most managers prefer to speak directly to a person within the same room. The manager has a greater chance to evaluate a candidate's professional appearance and personality.

## Group Interview

A group interview is where a manager interviews more than one person at the same time. This interview method is usually used by hiring managers with a high unfulfilled quota. The manager in a group interview has a chance to evaluate multiple candidates at the same time in one room. Most of the general group interview questions require an answer from every candidate in the room. A hiring specialist will evaluate each person's ability to answer their questions, professional appearance, and assertiveness.

## Group Interview Step by Step Instructions

1) Schedule 2 to 20 individuals to meet on a specific location, time, and date.

2) This step involves creating a evaluation sheet to grade the group being interview. The evaluation sheet is consisted of a list of names, comment boxes for each individual, and a variety of scoring boxes. The scoring boxes judge each individual base on their ability to volunteer, assertiveness, presentation, and personality. The grading method is usually 1 to 10 with 1 being bad and 10 being good.

3) Create a circle of desks and chairs. You will sit with the interviewers while forming the circle. The circle allows you to be part of the group instead in front of the group.

4) Ask everyone around the room to state their name and something about themselves. This is a great ice breaker to make everyone in the room more relaxed. You will be able to tell who's assertive and who is shy during this practice. This step will allow you to learn a little bit about every individual's personality.

5) Ask the group: Why are you guys here? This is a good opportunity for the group to express their personal and career goals.

6) Ask the group: What was your most favorite experience in your last job?

7) Ask the group: What was your worst experience in your last job?

8) Ask the group: Did you enjoy working with your last boss? If not then why?

9) Ask the group: Can you think of a time when you provide excellent customer service?

10) Ask the group: Can you think of a time when you received excellent customer service?

11) Ask the group: What can you offer to my company?

12) The next step is to give everyone a break while you check your evaluation sheets. You should be able to pick the best candidates and eliminate the nonqualified candidates.

13) The final step is to invite each individual separately into a closed room. You will schedule the qualified candidates to show up on another day for employment processing. The nonqualified candidates should be told the following: We will call you between 1- 2 days if you got the job. This sounds cruel, but it is for your own safety. Some candidates may become too angry with your decision and may cause harm to you.

These questions will evaluate the assertiveness of each individual. You will notice that the confident candidates will volunteer to answer your questions. The candidates that do not answer any of your questions are considered not suitable to be hired. You want to hire the best candidates and the group interview is a great method in determining who's qualified and who is not. The answers to these questions must be professional. You must understand that some of these questions do not apply to everyone in the group interview. The questions certain past work experiences should not apply to a person without experience. You should not count out an inexperience person immediately because they may have more unique or useful skills compared to an experience person. This situation is rare, but it can happen. Some managers may take an inexperience person and start them in a training or entry level program. Every individual has to start somewhere. If you have the ability to provide an individual with an opportunity then you should do it. You should remember that all your decisions and questions should follow your company's regulations to avoid causing problems.

## Proper Management

Most managers are given the job title and responsibilities because they have proved themselves. It is true that some managers may just delegate and not do anything themselves. Every manager and employee at a company has a responsibility. The employees must follow the directions established by their manager. The manager is responsible for delegating and maintaining the activities produced by their employees. The work place is an environment where everyone must work. It is important for both managers and employees to see more than one view. We will discuss examples and perspectives from both a manager and an employee.

### *Good versus Bad Manager*

Good Manager: **GM**
Bad Manager: **BM**

1) **GM:** Will provide one on training with a new hired employee.
   **BM:** Prefers new hired employees to be trained by other employees.

2) **GM:** Will immediately help an employee who may need assistance.

   **BM:** Chooses to ignore the employee and goes on with their other duties.

3) **GM:** Will give you an explanation about why you weren't given a promotion.

   **BM:** Will tell you that you didn't receive a promotion without any explanation.

These examples reflect the differences between a good manager and a bad manager. The good manager practices good business ethics by following company policy and providing assistance to their employees. A bad manager is a person who delegates without providing any assistance themselves. Here is a scenario that displays decisions from both a good manager and a bad manager:

*Good versus Bad Manager Scenario*

Steven works at a local home improvement store as a cashier. He was having a quiet day until a customer came up to him with a drill. The customer tells Steven that the drill is brand new. Steven inspects the drill and notices a great amount of wear and tear. The drill bits were worn out and the drill model is two years old. Steven realizes that the store does not even carry that same drill model since it is outdated. He decides to inform the customer that the item appears to be used and is outdated. The customer responds in a furious tone that he did indeed purchase item at the store and demands his money. Steven explains that the item is about two years old, which violates the company's return policy of less than 90 days. The customer in a response to Steven's comment demanded to speak with a manager. Steven calls up his manager to handle the situation.

**Good Manager's Decision:** A good manager would support Steven's ability to recognize and enforce the company's return policy. The good manager in this case would apologize and refuse the customer's request to return the drill.

**Bad Manager's Decision:** A bad manager would take the drill and refund the customer's money. This decision would give the customer an upper hand while Steven tried hard to defend the company's policy. Steven as the employee may feel discouraged from defending the company's return policy in the future. The manager must follow and enforce the company's policy. There are many reasons why a company would have a return policy. The return policy can save the company from losing money by restricting the customer's ability to return items. It is true that some customers like the one in this example will attempt to technically steal from a business. The customer obviously in this scenario wanted to return an old item that was used in multiple projects over a two year period. The company loses money by taking back an item that cannot be resold to the public or refunded by the manufacturer.

If you are a manager then you must remember to evaluate your decisions before making them. A good manager always analyzes their environment and solutions before making a final decision. You should always look at both sides of a situation to avoid establishing inaccurate decisions. A bad decision has a greater chance of producing inaccurate results. It is recommended for both managers and employees to view each other's positions before making a judgment.

## <u>Chapter Ten</u>

# Go out and apply what you learned

# Chapter Ten

# Go out and apply what you learned

I hope the contents and examples in this book will assist you in making effective decisions. You may use the contents from this book as a reference in your personal, academic, and career related decisions. This book was meant to build confidence and improve your decision making skills. The application of critical thinking can assist you in producing both accurate and effective decisions. You can improve your ability to gain success by engaging in each of the vital steps of critical thinking. It is important to realize that the processes of critical thinking only apply to situations that do not have a time restriction. The critical thinking process requires an extended amount of time to identify a problem, produce a plan, produce various solutions, and make a final decision. The examples in this book reflected the planning procedures and methods from the critical thinking process. I wish you luck in applying critical thinking and my examples in your future decisions.

www.ingramcontent.com/pod-product-compliance
Lightning Source LLC
Chambersburg PA
CBHW020253290526
45784CB00003B/1225